P

Level

SRa

Specific Skill Series

Working Within Words

Richard A. Boning

Fifth Edition

SRA/McGraw-Hill

Columbus, Ohio

SRA/McGraw-Hill

A Division of The McGraw·Hill Companies

Printed in the United States of America.

Send all inquiries to:
SRA/McGraw-Hill
8787 Orion Place
Columbus, OH 43240-4027

ISBN 0-02-687920-4

5 6 7 IPC 03 02 01

To the Teacher

PURPOSE:
WORKING WITHIN WORDS helps pupils put sounds and other word elements to work to determine word meaning. Many units in WORKING WITHIN WORDS develop understandings about sound-symbol (phonic) associations. Other units treat letter combinations, syllabication, roots and affixes, accent patterns, compound words, longer words, and spelling changes caused by adding endings.

FOR WHOM:
The skill of WORKING WITHIN WORDS is developed through a series of books spanning ten levels (Picture, Preparatory, A, B, C, D, E, F, G, H). The Picture Level is for pupils who have not acquired a basic sight vocabulary. The Preparatory Level is for pupils who have a basic sight vocabulary but are not yet ready for the first-grade-level book. Books A through H are appropriate for pupils who can read on levels one through eight, respectively. **The use of the *Specific Skill Series Placement Test* is recommended to determine the appropriate level.**

THE NEW EDITION:
The fifth edition of the *Specific Skill Series* maintains the quality and focus that has distinguished this program for more than 25 years. A key element central to the program's success has been the unique nature of the reading selections. Nonfiction pieces about current topics have been designed to stimulate the interest of students, motivating them to use the comprehension strategies they have learned to further their reading. To keep this important aspect of the program intact, a percentage of the reading selections have been replaced in order to ensure the continued relevance of the subject material.

In addition, a significant percentage of the artwork in the program has been replaced to give the books a contemporary look. The cover photographs are designed to appeal to readers of all ages.

SESSIONS:
Short practice sessions are the most effective. It is desirable to have a practice session every day or every other day, using a few units each session.

SCORING:
Pupils should record their answers on the reproducible worksheets. The worksheets make scoring easier and provide uniform records of the pupils' work. Using worksheets also avoids consuming the exercise books.

To the Teacher

It is important for pupils to know how well they are doing. For this reason, units should be scored as soon as they have been completed. Then a discussion can be held in which pupils justify their choices. (The Integrated Language Activities, many of which are open-ended, do not lend themselves to an objective score; thus there are no answer keys for these pages.)

GENERAL INFORMATION ON *WORKING WITHIN WORDS*:

The units are of two types: concept builders and functional exercises. The concept units focus the reader's attention on common patterns and parts of words. Each generalization is built step-by-step on the structure of previously formed concepts. The functional exercises either follow the concept units or are contained within them. They provide the reader with many immediate and repeated experiences with words involving particular patterns or principles. Sentence settings are typical for the pupils' level; often the choices offered are new words.

As WORKING WITHIN WORDS progresses through different word elements there is constant reinforcement. The more elementary booklets focus on phonic elements such as consonant sounds, consonant substitutions, blends, phonograms, and vowel sounds. As the level of difficulty increases, the emphasis shifts to syllabication, prefixes, suffixes, and roots.

A unit-by-unit list of concepts developed in this book is found on page 64.

INSTRUCTIONS:

Minimal direction is required. Pupils' attention must be drawn to the answer choices. In the concept units only two or three answer choices are offered. In the units that provide application of understandings, four to nine answer choices are offered, providing more experiences with words of a particular pattern. In units which offer an *F* choice, the *F* stands for NONE. This means that none of the choices makes sense in that particular setting.

RELATED MATERIALS:

Specific Skill Series Placement Tests, which enable the teacher to place pupils at their appropriate levels in each skill, are available for the Elementary (Pre-1–6) and Midway (4–8) grade levels.

About This Book

One of the first things you learned in school was the alphabet. You know the name of each letter in the alphabet. You know that written words are made up of these letters.

As you learn to read, you learn the sounds that letters stand for in words. First, you look at the letters in a word. Next, you put together the sounds of the letters. Then you can tell what the word is.

You can think of a word as a kind of secret message written in code. And you are a spy trying to find the meaning of that secret message. You are trying to **decode** the word. The sounds the letters stand for are the key to unlocking the code.

In this book, you will look at four pictures on a page. You will say the name for each picture. Then you will read four sentences. Each sentence has a blank. The word that goes in the blank is the name of one of the pictures. For some pages, the letter that stands for the **first** sound in the picture name is given as a clue. For other pages, the letter that stands for the **last** sound in the picture name is given as a clue. The word *monkey* begins with the letter *m*. The word *leaf* ends with the letter *f*. If you know the sounds that letters stand for, you will get the right answers.

When you know the sounds that letters stand for, you will have a key to reading. You will be able to unlock the meaning of written words.

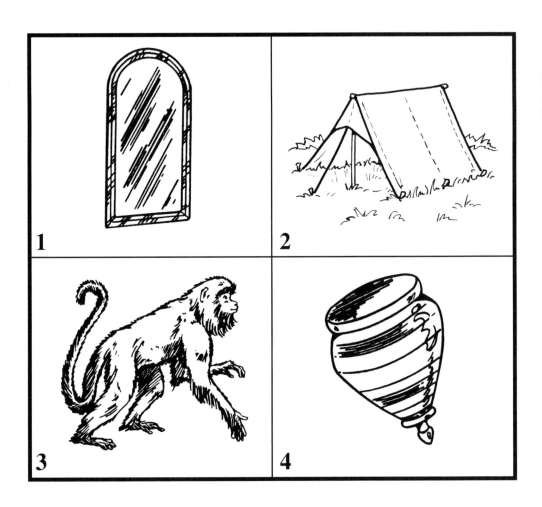

1. That **m**_____ likes to run.

2. We will go into the **t**_____ .

3. Jenny played with a **t**_____ .

4. Look in the **m**_____ .

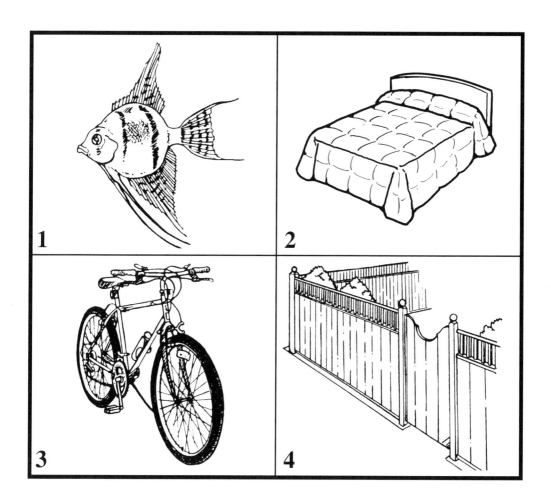

1. Father went to **b**_____.

2. The **f**_____ is in the water.

3. Can you jump the **f**_____?

4. I can ride a **b**_____.

1. Jenny has a pet **t**_____.

2. She is a little **b**_____.

3. Call me on the **t**_____.

4. I read a good **b**_____.

1. Thank you for the **f**_____.

2. Do not play with **m**_____.

3. The **f**_____ will make me cool.

4. Father is a big **m**_____.

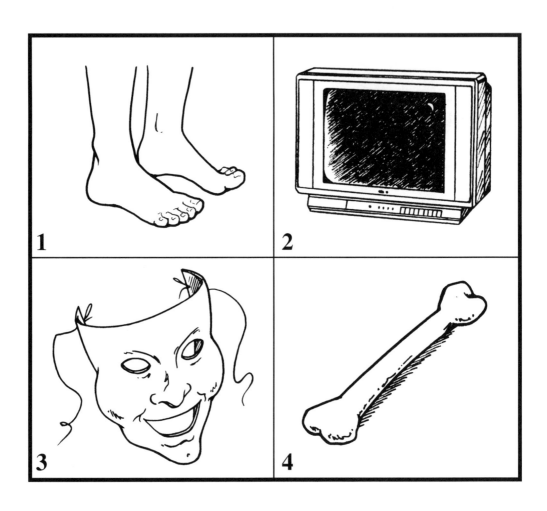

1. Bill likes to look at **t**_____.

2. Your **f**_____ are wet.

3. The **b**_____ is for my dog.

4. That is a funny **m**_____.

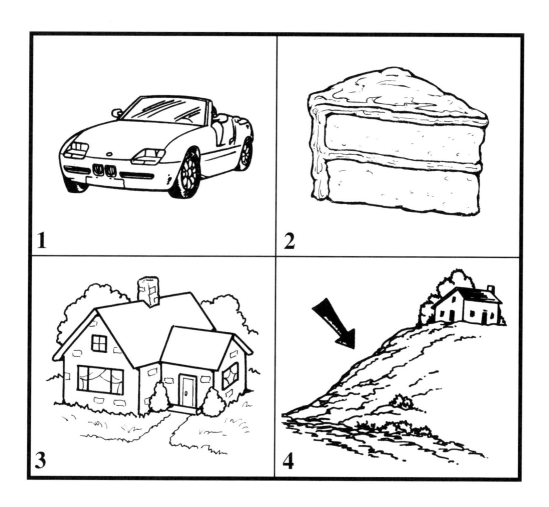

1. Pat is in the **h**_____.

2. Can you walk up that **h**_____?

3. Mother has a new **c**_____.

4. May I have some **c**_____?

1. I saw a **l**_____ at the zoo.

2. That man is a **s**_____.

3. There are **s**_____ cakes in the box.

4. The **l**_____ is green.

1. She can ride a **h**_____.

2. Pat is up on a **l**_____.

3. Ken has a new **h**_____.

4. I will read the **l**_____.

1. My **c**_____ ran away.

2. I have one **s**_____ .

3. Can you read the **s**_____?

4. May I eat the **c**_____?

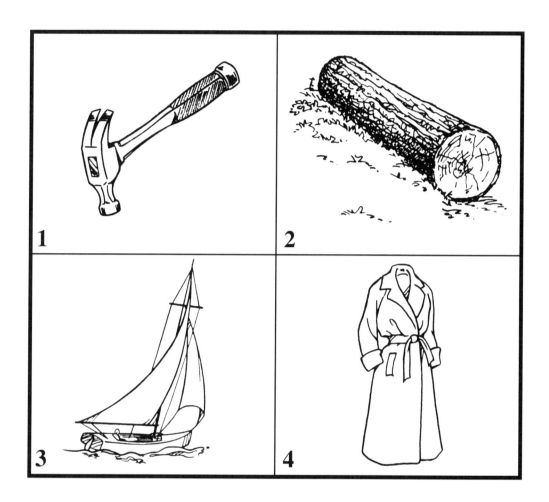

1. Mother works with a **h**_____.

2. Jenny sat on a **l**_____.

3. My **c**_____ is too big.

4. Put the **s**_____ in the water.

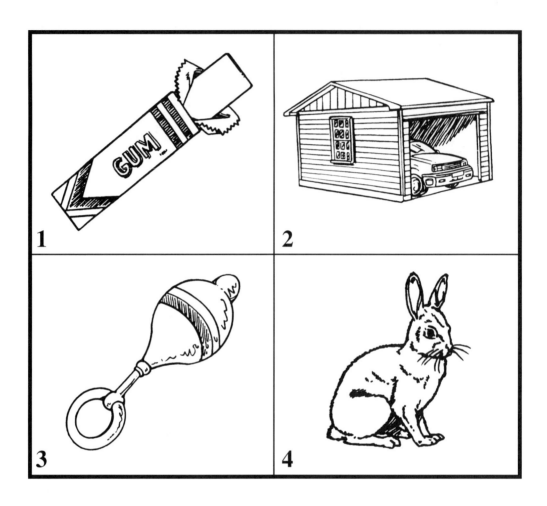

1. The car is in the **g**_____.

2. The baby has a new **r**_____.

3. Mother gave me some **g**_____.

4. Ann has a pet **r**_____.

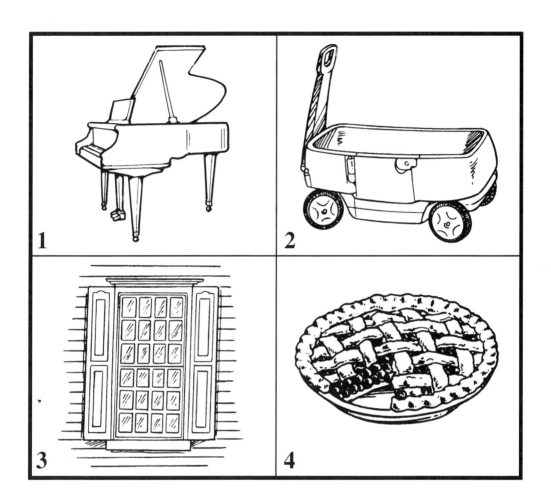

1. Can you play the **p**_____?

2. I like to eat **p**_____.

3. Look out the **w**_____.

4. Come ride in my **w**_____.

A. Exercising Your Skill

Name each picture below. Listen to the beginning sound. Write the letter that stands for the beginning sound.

List one word that names something in a kitchen and begins with the same sound as the thing in picture 1.

List one word that names something in a kitchen and begins with the same sound as the thing in picture 2.

B. Expanding Your Skill

Work with a partner. See how many things you can name that go in a kitchen. Write their names or draw them. Circle any ones that begin with the same sounds as the things in the pictures.

C. Exploring Language

Make alphabet soup. Copy the circle and the letters inside it. Then add these letters in the correct spots to make food names:

m   b   c   p

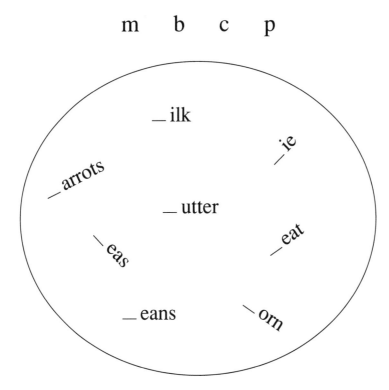

— ilk

— ie

— arrots

— utter

— eat

— eas

— eans

— orn

D. Expressing Yourself

Share a recipe with a friend. Pick something you like to eat. List all the things you need to make it. Then tell how to make it.

1. A **w**_____ came to my house.

2. A car went down the **r**_____.

3. Sam got wet in the **r**_____.

4. Paint the **w**_____ blue.

1. Ann worked in the **g**_____.

2. Put the **p**_____ on the bed.

3. That **g**_____ can read.

4. Put some water in the **p**_____.

1. Can you hear the **r**_____?

2. She has a new **w**_____.

3. The **p**_____ likes to eat.

4. That is a big **g**_____.

1. Please ring the **d**_____.

2. He is a **k**_____.

3. We eat in the **k**_____.

4. A **d**_____ can run fast.

1. Daddy likes to read the **n**_____.

2. Judy wants to be a **n**_____.

3. Wash your hands in the **s**_____.

4. Bill has a new **s**_____.

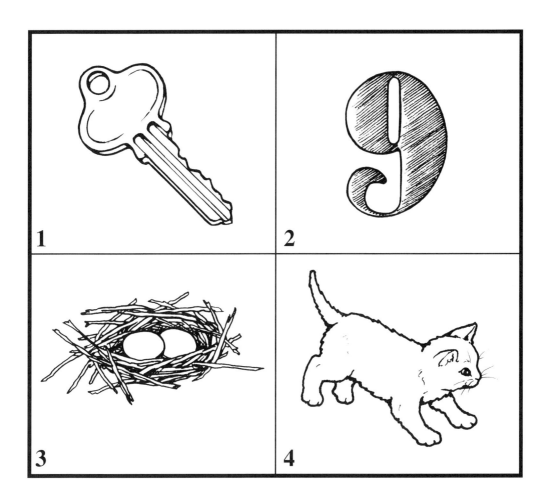

1. Ann's pet is a **k**_____.

2. A **n**_____ is in the tree.

3. N_____ boys played ball.

4. I have a **k**_____ to my house.

1. My **d**_____ is named Sam.

2. Dan works with a **s**_____.

3. Do you like to eat **d**_____?

4. The **s**_____ is far away.

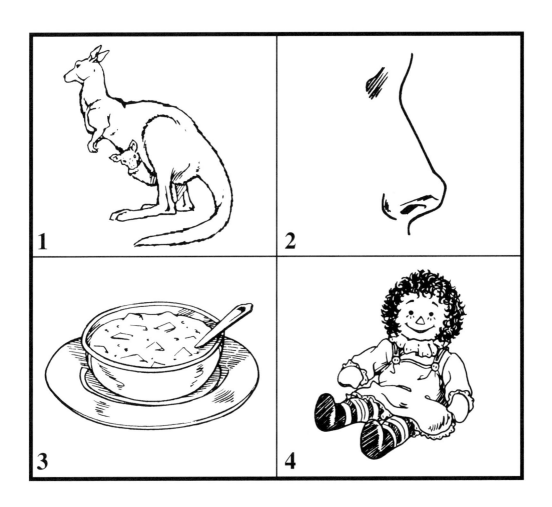

1. Meg likes to eat **s**_____.

2. A **k**_____ is at the zoo.

3. Mother gave me a new **d**_____.

4. My **n**_____ is cold.

1. Jill has a pet **m**_____.

2. The **c**_____ can go fast.

3. Put on your **c**_____.

28

4. That **m**_____ has a boat.

1. My **h**_____ is painted green.

2. The book is on the **t**_____.

3. I like your **h**_____ and coat.

4. Did you hear the **t**_____?

1. May I read your l_____?

2. Did you cut your l_____?

3. My dog has a big b_____.

4. Ann has a new b_____.

1. They put out the **f**_____.

2. Use the **s**_____ and the water.

3. Mother made **s**_____ to eat.

4. Tom ran with the **f**_____.

A. Exercising Your Skill

Look at the pictures. Add the missing letter to each sentence.

I go to school on a __us.　　I sit at my __esk.
I take a seat near the　　It is by the __oor.
　__ack.

B. Expanding Your Skill

Play "I spy." Think of the name of a thing in the room. Tell the beginning sound. See who can guess what word you are thinking of. Give one point for each correct guess.

Use these beginning sounds:

b	l	w	g	n	s	c	t

C. Exploring Language

Add the missing letters to complete the story. Then think of one more sentence you could add.

Our teacher told a tale.

It was such a __illy story!

It was about a pink __ig named Pete.

He ran into our __oom.

He had a hat on his __ead.

He had big blue __oots on his feet.

D. Expressing Yourself

Draw a picture of the animal in the story above. Give the picture a name.

1. The **d**_____ on the house is new.

2. The car is in the **g**_____.

3. Do you know that **g**_____?

4. My **d**_____ ran away.

1. Bill's **k**_____ likes to play.

2. This **r**_____ goes to my house.

3. Can you fly a **k**_____?

4. Look at the **r**_____ jump.

1. Juan painted the **w**＿＿＿＿ blue.

2. That **w**＿＿＿＿ is my mother.

3. Did you read the **n**＿＿＿＿?

4. I have **n**＿＿＿＿ books.

1. Put on your blue **s**_____ .

2. That **p**_____ is fat.

3. What is in the **p**_____ ?

4. Tell me what the **s**_____ says.

1. Who gave the baby the **r**_____?

2. Put on the funny **m**_____.

3. Do not eat the **g**_____.

4. We have a new **t**_____.

1. Look at the **k**_____.

2. May I have some **p**_____?

3. Turn on the **f**_____.

4. The house is made of **w**_____.

1. Look at the **d**_____.

2. I have a pet **c**_____.

3. She can ride a **h**_____.

4. Do not jump on the **b**_____.

1. The man put on his **v**_____.

2. We saw a lion at the **z**_____.

3. That woman is the **qu**_____.

4. I like to play with the **y**_____.

1. May I ride in the _____**t**?

2. That house has a new _____**f**.

3. Put on your _____**f**.

4. My _____**t** jumped on my bed.

1. I saw cows at the _____**m**.

2. Mother rides on a _____**s**.

3. Can you play that _____**m**?

4. Fill the _____**s** with milk.

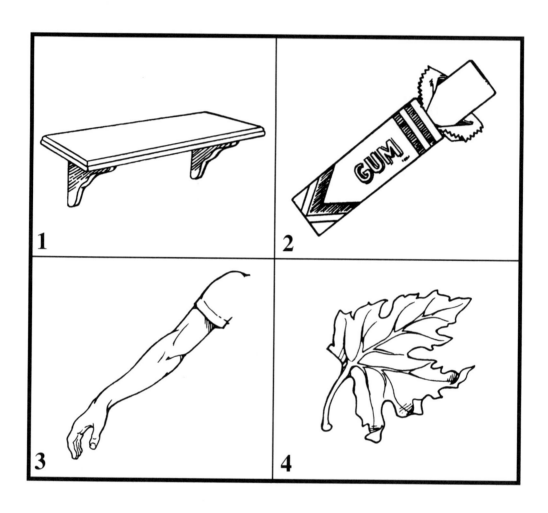

1. Put the book on the _____f.

2. This _____f is from that tree.

3. Do not eat the _____m.

4. Did he fall and cut his _____m?

1. Put it in the _____t.

2. Try on your new _____s.

3. Do not fall down the _____s.

4. The _____t is Jill's pet.

1. I saw Pat on the _____s.

2. My cat is up on the _____f.

3. We stayed in a _____t.

4. The fish ate the _____m.

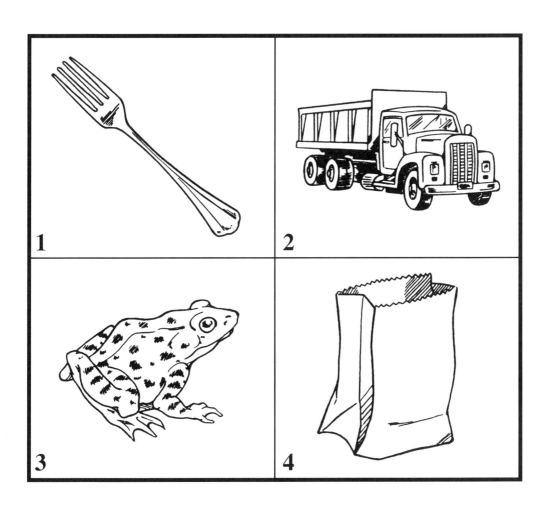

1. My pet _____g can jump far.

2. I will eat this with a _____k.

3. I have a _____g of toys.

4. Did you ride in the _____k?

A. Exercising Your Skill

Name each picture. Listen to the end sound. Write the missing letter in each word.

ca＿   do＿

Now add the missing letters to make animal names.

I am bigger than a mouse. I am a ra＿.
I can wiggle in the dirt. I am a wor＿.
I swim and I fly. I am a duc＿.

B. Expanding Your Skill

Play "heads and tails." Write an animal name. Cut it apart. Mix up the parts with parts from three classmates. Swap papers with another group and put the animal names together again.

C. Exploring Language

Read these sentences. Add the missing letters.

A fro__ can hop on a log.

A __orse can kic__ with its hoofs.

A snake can his__, but it cannot kis__.

A __ird can tweet a sweet song.

A pi__ grows very big.

D. Expressing Yourself

Do one of these things.

1. Sing "Old MacDonald Had a Farm." When you get to the name of a new animal, say only the beginning sound. Let your classmates guess its name.

2. Draw and color four animals. Cut them apart. See if a classmate can put the heads and tails back together.

1. A _____p is a big boat.

2. That cat has a long _____l.

3. This _____l is for a bike.

4. I saw a _____p at the zoo.

1. A _____l ran up the tree.

2. Look at the _____g eat.

3. The girls played _____l.

4. The baby played on the _____g.

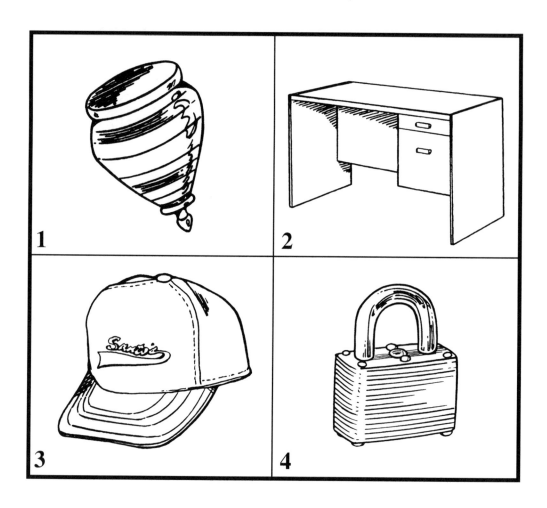

1. Bob sat at his _____**k**.

2. Can you open this _____**k**?

3. Put your _____**p** on.

4. A _____**p** is a good toy.

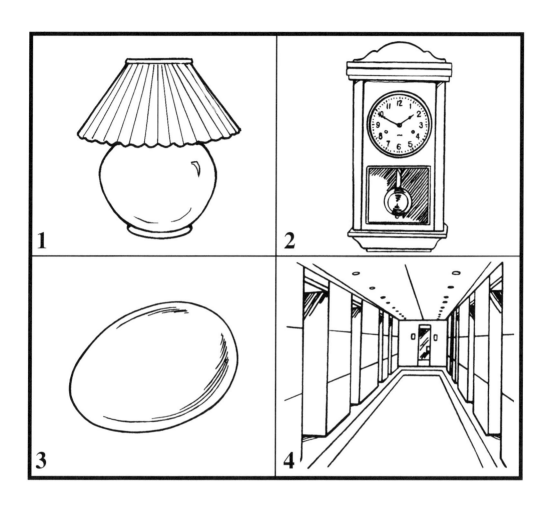

1. May I eat the _____**g**?

2. We have a new _____**p**.

3. Mother walked down the _____**l**.

4. A _____**k** tells time.

1. She is a _____**r**.

2. The _____**n** is funny.

3. The baby eats with a _____**n**.

4. Sit on the _____**r**.

1. My house is made of _____**d**.

2. A _____**k** likes the rain.

3. She got a new _____**d**.

4. May I read your _____**k**?

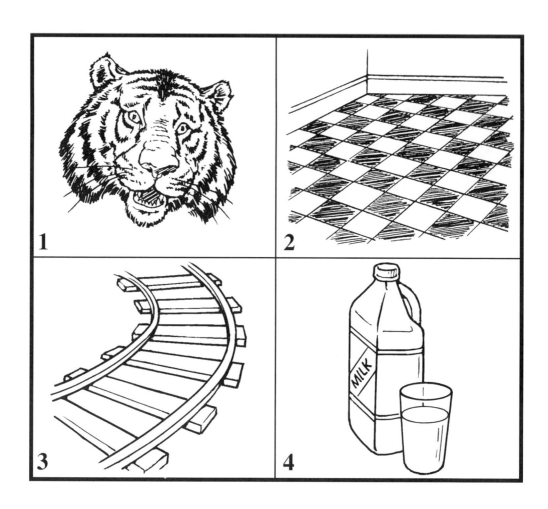

1. Give the baby some _____**k**.

2. The girls sat on the _____**r**.

3. That _____**r** is not a pet.

4. Put the train on the _____**k**.

1. We have _____**n** books.

2. The cake is in the _____**n**.

3. I see a _____**d** in the tree.

4. Meg plays in the _____**d**.

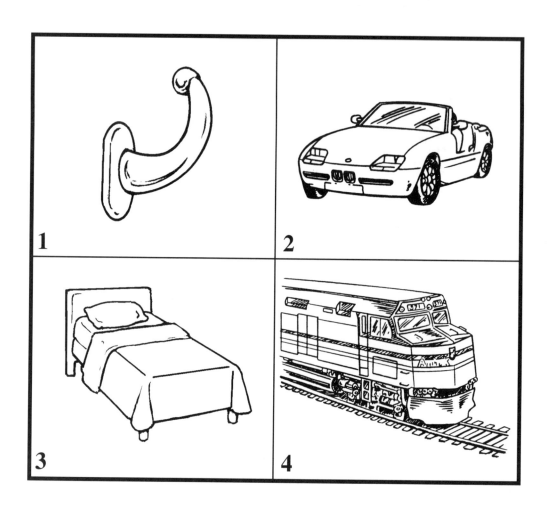

1. The _____**r** went down the road.

2. Do not jump on your _____**d**.

3. The coat is on a _____**k**.

4. Ann has a toy _____**n**.

1. See the baby _____**k**!

2. The _____**t** is big.

3. You have a little _____**g**.

4. Pat has a new _____**f**.

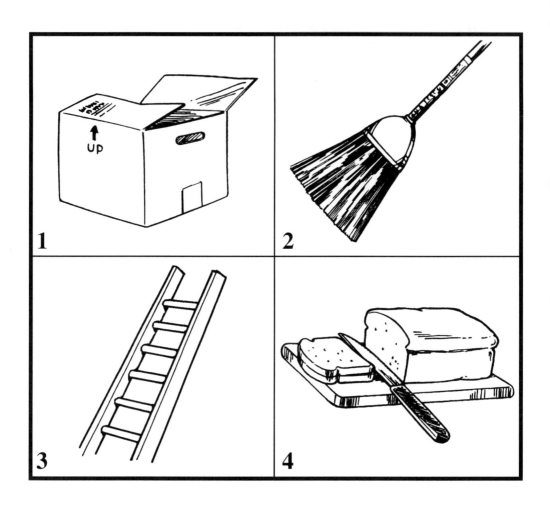

1. May I have some _____**d**?

2. Put the toys in the _____**x**.

3. Who has my _____**m**?

4. Will you go up that _____**r**?

1. May I play with your _____l?

2. We looked at the _____p.

3. Sam has a pet _____k.

4. The cows are in the _____n.

A. Exercising Your Skill

Read the signs that go on this road. Think about the end sounds. Add the missing letters.

Exi__

Sto__

No Left Tur__

B. Expanding Your Skill

Make a list of other signs you have seen. Think about signs on roads, signs at school, and signs on stores.

Leave the end letter off each sign. See if your classmates can add the correct letter.

Compare your signs with those of your classmates. How many different ones do you have in all?

C. Exploring Language

Look at the arrows. Add the end sound to each word to show what the arrows mean.

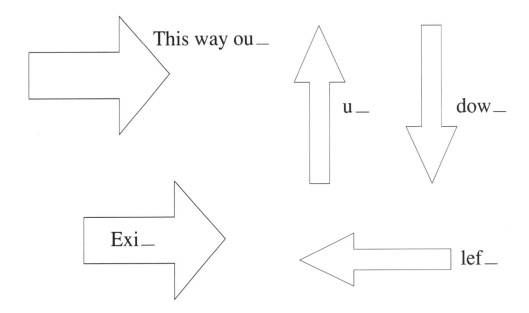

This way ou_

u_

dow_

Exi_

lef_

D. Expressing Yourself

Draw and color a sign you have seen. Think about why we need this sign. Tell your class about it.

CONCEPTS DEVELOPED